MATT,

THANK

THOUGHTS,

PRAYERS IN HELPING LINDA

AND I COMPLETE THIS JOURNEY,

AARON

I Do—I Did

My Fifteen-Year Journey of Caring for
My Wife with Early-Onset Alzheimer's

P. AARON LESKO

WESTBOW
PRESS®
A DIVISION OF THOMAS NELSON
& ZONDERVAN

WestBow Press books may be ordered through booksellers or by contacting:

WestBow Press
A Division of Thomas Nelson & Zondervan
1663 Liberty Drive
Bloomington, IN 47403
www.westbowpress.com
844-714-3454

ISBN: 978-1-6642-0569-7 (sc)
ISBN: 978-1-6642-0570-3 (hc)
ISBN: 978-1-6642-0568-0 (e)

Library of Congress Control Number: 2020918065

Print information available on the last page.

WestBow Press rev. date: 09/29/2020

CONTENTS

ACKNOWLEDGMENTS

I wish to express my appreciation of my daughter, Christine Tyson, for her valuable editing and comments regarding this project. It was difficult for her, given that the book's subject is her mother's life and passing, but we pressed on together.

I also wish to thank Angie and Gina for making lots of noise in the beginning to encourage me to get going in writing this book. Without their "forceful" encouragement, I do not know if it ever would have happened.

Also, there are so many friends who supported me in this care-giving journey; the list is too long to recount here. The ones who helped firsthand and the many others who helped from a distance all contributed in priceless ways. God bless them one and all.

Lastly, I so appreciate my family members who supported me in my journey and contributed to this book by being examples of a wonderful and supportive family.

Linda Kay Lesko, June 6, 1950 – December 3, 2015

"Christian, mother of three, grandmother,
musician, vocalist, journalist, English
teacher, home maker, my soul mate
and dear wife of 43 years"

INTRODUCTION

After Linda's passing, a number of family members and friends suggested that I write a book reflecting on my caregiving for my wife. Initially, I thought it not worth the effort. After all, there are many books on such topics. Why add another one?

As I reflected on the fifteen years I cared for my wife, I thought of other stories and events that I could have mentioned in the tribute I gave her at her funeral. I wished I had kept a journal of all our years together, as my memory is not good enough to recall everything. I kept rehearsing remembered events in my mind until one day, the obvious thought occurred to me: *Maybe I should write about them in a book.* If nothing else, recounting all these events would help me heal, even if I never published a book. And the book could be something for my grandchildren to reflect on.

So, I started to write. It flowed rather easily—one

story after another and one thought after another. Before long, a book began emerging. To be honest, writing it was very emotional at times. Tears flowed as I remembered heavy details. Some healing was taking place.

I am glad I wrote this book. I can only hope and pray that others glean from it too. I look for it to not only bless others but inspire them also in their caregiving. Our cultures today have lost much of what has built society. Caregiving gets delegated to institutions. Things like marriage, family, and care for others seems to have become less important than wealth and careers. So many people today are more self-centered than giving. And that is what the media glorifies.

However, through my experience, I have learned to not be critical of anyone. Everyone has their own set of circumstances. Not all people have the means or ability to care for others. But love in a relationship needs to be built up and kept strong. The commitment in a relationship should never be thrown away because the going gets difficult. I believe that there is an eternal purpose in doing whatever is laid before you in this life. When you serve others, you are serving God Himself.

Scripture references are mentioned throughout the book to relate my experiences with some of what God has to say about these life experiences. His Word, the Bible, is completely instructive for our lives.

PART 1

❦

Early On

Before Diagnosis

W e humans live life like nothing will ever go wrong. We take so much for granted. Such was the case for Linda and me when we were growing up.

Linda and I met in our church when she was ten and I was twelve. Both our families were of the Christian faith. Our relationships with our Lord were all encompassing for both of us.

We would enjoy each other's company every time our church youth group got together. Social events with the group were a time that cemented our friendship.

Linda and I seemed to hit it off, as they say. As you grow mutually comfortable with a friend, you sense that your friendship is becoming valuable. Such was the case with Linda and me. We grew into our relationship over many years. I was attracted to her, and she admitted later on that she, too, was attracted to me.

It was just a matter of time until we both recognized that our relationship was to be for a lifetime.

As our college years came, our relationship got more serious, and by the time she was a senior in college, we were committed to each other. I asked her to marry me. Life became routine once we married.

Linda had graduated cum laude from college with an English-teaching degree which enabled her to teach English in a Christian school. The school recognized her talent early on and offered her the position of department head, but she declined. At the time, she explained that she declined the offer because the job would be too much of a time commitment. That puzzled me. I now think that she declined it because she had begun to feel some kind of mental compromise. She was just thirty years old.

Early-onset Alzheimer's is so subtle. At first, the deterioration is so gradual that it appears to just be caused by aging. But the decline is so relentlessly steady that it becomes significant at some point.

If I had had more insight at the time, I would have inquired more about why she declined the department-head job. We, like other couples, tended to let each other have our own space. We each had a role, and we stayed out of each other's way.

That is not to say I did not care. We were both responsible and productive. We had plenty of distractions around us. We were busy with three children, family events, church activities, holidays, and birthdays. We had moved from a mobile home to a ranch-style house to a contemporary house in the suburbs, which we were decorating. We had careers. We enjoyed life. We had much responsibility, and together, we were succeeding. There seemed to be no need to dig any deeper.

No one dreamed that a terminal illness was looming. No one ever does. We humans all live like death is decades away, as we should. But I think we need to learn the lesson that establishing an open and intimate relationship and keeping communication strong in that relationship sets an effective stage for whatever is to come. It gives us the ability to deal with reality more freely, more thoroughly, and more comfortably as partners. You should have no barrier, intentional or not, to self-expression. Stay both quick and able to discuss any nuances of life because you never know what is ahead. Normalcy is not guaranteed in this life.

As the next twenty years went by, Linda's career got continuously leaner. She went from being an English teacher to a journalist for the city paper to a journalist for a local township paper. By the time she was forty, she could no longer reconcile a bank statement. Here was a mind that earned A's in college calculus but now could no longer do arithmetic. Something was wrong, and she and I simply accepted it because she could still function as a person and a mother and a housewife. We certainly did not expect that she had a life-threatening illness.

While there was and still is no cure, I think I would have started caring for her in other ways if I had known then what I know now. I should have had conversations with her concerning her decline. Being the strong person she was, she never let on that she was compromised. She just accepted it and adjusted her lifestyle to accommodate it. She lived within her mental means. But it must have been uncomfortable and maybe even frightening at times. I regret not inquiring, not conversing, not facing reality, not hearing her describe her state.

The Day I Admitted
Something Was Wrong

O ne day in the year 2000, after I came home from work, I sat on the couch, and Linda sat next to me. (I still miss that companionship.) There, she began to recount a story of something that had happened during her day. Then a minute later, she told me the exact same story as if she had never told it. Then she told the story a third time, again as if for the first time. In that moment, I knew that something was very wrong. It was not like her, being a cum laude graduate from college. Linda was too smart and full of life to make that mistake.

Now that I know what I know, I realize things like that had been going on for a long time, maybe not such obvious things, but little signs. She would forget things from time to time. She could no longer do some simple things that many of us do routinely. Ten years earlier, she had begun struggling to reconcile bank statements. I had ignored what was wrong. In many cases like this, you often do not think the worst. You just think what is wrong does not matter that much, so you ignore it. You live with it and chalk it up to a bad day or something inconsequential, but this sign was too obvious.

When I told her that she had just told me the same story three times, Linda simply hung her head. I told her that we needed to have her checked medically. She was silent. I think she knew that something was very wrong. I put my arms around her and held her tight.

The next day, I called our family doctor and told him that Linda was having memory issues. He said it could be just a vitamin deficiency, and I should bring her in for blood work. The test came back negative— no deficiency—so he referred us to a neurologist.

Then, the long and arduous journey started. We had many tests done. You see, at the time of this writing you cannot test for Alzheimer's. You have to test for everything else you *can* test for. If the tests all come back negative, then you can assume it is Alzheimer's, but doing all those tests takes many months. In our case, it took over a year.

All the medical tests came back negative. Finally, we had a genetic test done. That test was most significant to me. With all her previous negative test results and her genetic markers, the results said that there was a 93 percent chance that she had Alzheimer's. My heart sank as I read the report. My dear wife had probable Alzheimer's. With her failing mental state, it was obvious, and, in time, it was confirmed even more so as she continued to deteriorate cognitively.

One of Linda's last psychological tests confirmed that the right frontal lobe of her brain, where arithmetic is processed, was being attacked. Remember, she had gotten A's in college calculus, and now, she could no longer add two and two to get four. Linda was losing her thinking and reasoning ability. The psychologist who administered the test said that those at this stage of her condition would live ten to twenty years more. She was just fifty years old.

By the time Linda turned fifty and was diagnosed with probable Alzheimer's, the disease had done a lot of damage. But she had a long list of accomplishments for someone who was only able to be productive for half a normal lifetime. I often wonder what she would have accomplished had she lived a normal life span.

As we walked out of the psychologist's office, Linda said, "I shall never see my grandchildren become adults," and then she put her face in her hands and cried. I held her tight as we sobbed together. There was no comforting her to soften that news. It was devastating.

She knew early on that the prognosis was grim. Not long after that day, she asked me if I would take care of her as her condition deteriorated. I could not have meant it more as I told her of course I would. I said that I would always love her and always take care of her. And I meant it. I had said, "*I do*," when we took our vows, and now, it was time to see those vows through to the end, so *I did*.

The Admission of the Decline

T hree years after her diagnosis, Linda was still able to do many things, including driving. However, she had not done any evening driving, until one day when she had to come home late. Somehow, the darkness hampered her ability to see and judge what was going on. As she was driving home, she went through a stop sign, and a truck rammed into the side of her car.

When I went home that evening and she was not there, I started to worry. As the evening went on, I knew that something was very wrong. I started to make phone calls when an emergency-room staff member called me to tell me Linda was there at the hospital. She had had a concussion during the accident, so an ambulance had taken her to the hospital. I picked her up and brought her home. Her car had been towed away and had to be totaled.

Linda's driving had been deteriorating for some months. Unfortunately, I had waited too long to tell her to stop driving, and that had resulted in a bad accident, thank God with no serious consequences. Looking back, I should have stopped her from driving sooner. It is always difficult to tell someone in our society to stop driving, as it is a loss of independence. Convincing someone who is ill to stop driving is especially hard; they think they can still do everything because they cannot judge their abilities very well anymore. You have to be proactive for their safety and the safety of others.

Following this serious accident, I did stop Linda from driving. She became homebound and for a time was not happy about it. Imagine going from being 100 percent free to being stuck in a house. After some months of this, Linda wandered out of the house when I was not there. Someone called the police as they noticed her wandering the streets. The police had an ambulance take her home, and then, they called me. I was frightened by all of this and imagined how bad it could have turned out if no one had spotted Linda. That is when I started having her supervised. She could no longer be left alone.

When you are caring for someone who has a life-threatening illness, it is important that you look ahead and manage the situation with people's safety in mind. That means you must face up to where things are headed and take proactive steps. That is easier said than done.

I was surprised by how quickly Linda's condition worsened. The deterioration seemed to accelerate in those few years. It was not too long before she could no longer care for herself.

One day, she could use a fork, and a few weeks later, she had to eat using her hands. In a few more weeks, I had to feed her.

One day, she could talk, and soon, she no longer could express any words.

One day, she could dress herself, and soon, she simply did not know how to anymore.

One day, she could prepare a meal, and soon, she did not even know what the kitchen was for.

One day, she could climb a flight of steps, and soon, she would trip and fall over just one step in front of her.

One day, she could drink from a cup, and soon, I had to hold the cup while she sucked from a straw.

I became paranoid over every little detail of her

daily functioning. One simple ability after another disappeared with no end in sight until the day came when she collapsed to the floor because she could no longer balance herself or take a step. That was the day she became bedridden.

These transitions are always difficult. We watch babies develop into toddlers, then into adolescents, and so on. It takes some years for all this growth to take place. With Alzheimer's, it is the same process only in reverse. Imagine watching a perfectly normal and productive adult fall to a vegetative state in a handful of years. This deterioration is supposed to happen in one's elderly years, not in the middle of one's life.

Seeing Linda lose one ability after another frightened and saddened me. It would make me cry seeing her deteriorate right before my eyes, and every deterioration was a sad reminder of the inevitable. I learned to brace myself. I had to prepare for the worst because it was happening right before my eyes. These were times when I relied heavily on my Christian faith. These were times when only God's strength would suffice, and I asked for it frequently (Isaiah 41:13; Philippians 4:13).

PART 2

❦

Some Miracles
I Noticed

All I Did Was Cut the Grass

So often, we carry on with life routinely once we become caregivers. In one sense, it is important for us to do so in order to have some normalcy. However, we must also take into account that the one we are caring for has some limitations, and those limitations will be ever changing. Those limitations could be simple or extensive. I found it so hard to keep track of all of Linda's limitations. As good a job as I would do, from time to time, I would misjudge a situation or take a chance I should not have.

Cutting the grass on our riding lawn mower was a simple thing that I did every week throughout the summer. I just cut the grass. I thought nothing of it. It was my routine. One day, I told Linda that I would be outside cutting the grass. As far as I could tell, she fully understood me, at least in the moment. But with Alzheimer's, there is a memory problem. No matter what I told her, she did not remember it and certainly did not manage it.

While I was riding around the yard, I came to a corner of the house. I could not see around the corner. As it turned out, Linda was looking for me and stepped around that corner just as I approached it from the opposite side. I slammed on the brake and stopped just inches from her. The heavy riding lawn mower, with its spinning blades, would have done unforgivable damage to her.

To recount this incident causes me to shudder. I can only thank God that I was paying as much attention as I was. I believe His guardian angels saved Linda from a serious accident and me from heartache. From that time on, I only cut the grass when a caregiver was in the house supervising Linda. Somehow, we caregivers have to think ahead to what our lives will be like when things get further along with our loved one's condition. It is hard to think of everything, but making that effort is extremely important for avoiding accidents and other negative consequences.

I learned that day that I should look for Divine intervention. God cared for Linda and me in so many ways. All I had to do was notice them (Psalm 121:5–8).

A Miracle of Money

I had just turned the big 5-0 when, for no apparent reason, I thought I should buy long-term care insurance for Linda and myself. It was a relatively new idea in the insurance marketplace. I used to think I pursued long-term care insurance because I was feeling my age and planning for the long term. But I now know it was Divine intervention.

To my surprise, the first salesman I approached refused to sell the insurance to me, saying that I was too young. I suppose with that response, I should have delayed my pursuit of this insurance, but I didn't. More Divine intervention.

The second salesman I talked to was not so hesitant, so Linda and I went ahead and bought two policies from him, one for each of us. Just two years after I started paying the too-high premiums, Linda was diagnosed with probable Alzheimer's. She did not need daily care at that time, but I knew that day was not far off.

About four years after her diagnosis, Linda started to need supervision, so I tapped into the long-term care insurance. Today, long-term care policies are not so generous; they require that your loved one get certified care in a facility. But our policy was just right. I did need certified caregivers for Linda, but the policy said they could do their caregiving in our home. Divine intervention.

And so, the caring began. After some months of part-time care, the caregivers started coming to our home at eight thirty in the morning and leaving at six in the evening. That is what the daily allowance would pay for, so that is how the schedule was set. That gave me the ability to be out of the house or at work every day for those hours. And this was seven days a week. Sickness does not take any time off!

However, it was not cheap. After all the years of care for seven days a week, the final tally of all the bills was over $642,000. This total shocked me. Paying that kind of money would have required me to sell my house and then some. I know that paying these bills is what the insurance is for, and, also, that Divine intervention took care of that need.

As I have looked back over the journey of the last twenty years, I have realized that how it all worked out was a miracle. All too often, we take things in our lives as routine, but if we just ponder them for a while, more often than not, we will find God's hand at work in taking care of all the details in our lives. We may not like those details. After all, my wife was diagnosed with a long-term terminal illness. But He really is in control. He does not allow anything in our life path that we are incapable of coping with. We may not like what is happening, but it is there for a purpose. Accept that, and you will be all the better for it. Most of all, you will be serving His purpose, whatever that may be (Romans 8:28).

I Think I Met an Angel

I t had become a routine to go grocery shopping every week and buy the essential things that we needed for Linda's care as well as the needs for the house. It was like any family's grocery shopping with one exception: Linda's needs as a terminally ill member of the household.

One particular week, one of my grandsons went with me to Walmart to do my grocery shopping. By this time, Linda was bedridden and needed things like baby food, incontinence supplies, body lotion, and disposable things for the bedside. I knew the list well. I had done my shopping for these things many times. For me, it was routine.

When my grandson and I were done walking the isles, we entered the checkout line with our cart, put all our things on the conveyor belt, and waited. It was just another routine pile of supplies to us. As the cashier was ringing it all up, there was an elderly man bagging it all at the end of the checkout.

And then, the elderly man who was bagging our groceries asked my grandson why we had all these baby-food jars. I guess we did not look like we should have them. At the time, I was in my sixties, and my grandson was twelve. My grandson answered him matter-of-factly, "Oh, my Grammie has Alzheimer's, and this is all she can eat."

The man looked very concerned. He immediately stopped his bagging and walked over to me. He put his hand out to shake mine. As we shook hands, he looked into my eyes. I do not know how to describe his piercing gaze. It certainly was a look of concern and care.

And then, with tears in his eyes, he said, "When I go to church this weekend, I shall say prayers for you."

I cannot say that those words were profound. But with his very concerned gaze, I somehow knew that he knew what I was dealing with. It felt as if my heart stopped beating in that moment. Someone who was a complete stranger to me knew what I was going through. He took the moment to talk to me. He shook my hand. He looked at me very concerned. He cared and told me so.

Many times, after that day, I recounted my experience with him. It always comforted me to remember his simple words and his look of care and concern. Whenever I felt alone in my daily routine, I took strength from this one man's interest in me even though we were complete strangers. He showed me you never know how your encouraging words and deeds will affect someone, and you should never hesitate to be an encourager.

I had never noticed that man before, even though I had been in that store hundreds of times. And I have never seen him since. Whether he was really an angel or not, I do not know, but to me, he sure was (Hebrews 1:14).

I Was Silenced

B y my seventh year of caring for Linda, her quality of life had steadily declined. She had not spoken in a few years. She had to be fed. She was incontinent. She was getting close to not being ambulatory, but we were still able to attend church as a couple.

It was a cold winter Sunday morning in January during the seventh year of caring for her. I got her dressed, and off to church we went. I could tell her walk was getting weaker. It would not be long until she could no longer go outside. As it was, she could not keep up with my slow walking. We had to basically crawl along as she held my arm. I had become her teddy bear!

Finally, we climbed the church steps and went to the worship hall, a large room that could hold several hundred people. I helped her take off her coat as we took our seats. Soon, the worship leader asked us all to stand to sing and worship, as is the custom in our church.

Linda and I stood, and I joined in the singing. Linda could no longer do so; for the last few years, she had simply stood and remained silent during this time. But then …

I could not believe my ears. I heard her singing! Looking at Linda, I saw her singing notes of music that were in complete harmony, but she was not using any English words. As I watched and listened, I stopped singing. Hers was the most beautiful worship I had ever heard. I shed tears as I stood there seeing with my eyes, hearing with my ears, and finding it impossible to comprehend with my mind that she was worshipping in song. She had not uttered any sound in years but could worship God in a way that was beyond my ability.

Not only was I silenced, but I sensed that all the heavenly hosts were hushed as well as we all stood there listening to a human being worshipping God using notes of music and no English words. Scripture declares that if we humans did not worship God, then rocks would cry out in worship (Luke 19:37–40), and that took on a whole new meaning that day. Linda did not seem capable of any communication, but you simply cannot hold back worship when it is directed toward God. He enabled her worship even though it was "impossible" (Matthew 19:26).

That was the most beautiful worship I have ever heard. I do not think I shall ever hear the likes of it again until I, too, am in eternity.

He Said, "That's Too Bad"

Abbout ten years into my journey of caring for Linda, she was completely unresponsive. She had been bedridden for about three years. All she needed was basic care. All she could do was lie in her bed in the family room. When I looked at her and spoke to her, her eyes just stared right through me. For that reason, I rarely tried to engage her. It was too difficult. It was too sad. Anyone who looked at my situation from the outside understood well that it was quite an endeavor.

A couple who knew Linda and me well came to me and asked if they could bring dinner over once every week as well as visit to help me pass the time and encourage me. Others had made similar generous offers. I responded to this couple just as I had to all the others. I said no, for I knew that their involvement would be for years and very disruptive to their lives, as it had become to mine. My journey was not anywhere near the end, and I did not want anyone else to have to endure it. All the others who made such an offer understood my response and walked away, but not this couple.

As soon as I explained to him that it would be too burdensome for them, my friend responded to me firmly and immediately. He said, "That's too bad, because we are coming over anyway!" This stunned and silenced me. I had never heard such a response before, so I welcomed them. A long-term caregiver needs help always, even when they refuse it.

I talked these dear friends into coming every other week just to make it easier for them. So, they, along with another kind couple, brought over a home-cooked meal every other week. They not only brought the meal but ate it with me and spent several hours with me each time. I always looked forward to these evenings. The meals were delicious, the fellowship was enjoyable, and the ladies would also spend some time just talking to Linda, even though there was no response. At Christmastime, they stood around Linda's bed singing carols to her. Often, they would pray for her. Sometimes, we all would watch a movie in the same room that Linda was in. It was as close to normalcy as I could get. It felt comforting.

The couples continued to come in the last weeks and days of Linda's time here on earth. By this time, she was in hospice care. Now the prayers of these visits asked for her to be comfortable in her last days. It was a matter of days or weeks till she would be gone from this earth. As these dear friends gathered around Linda's bed to pray for her for what was the last time, I could not thank God enough for their involvement. It was beautiful to see these loving Christian friends doing what God had laid on their hearts.

The lesson for all of us is that when God lays a task on your heart, you better step up to the plate and make it happen even if there is pushback. May we all take a lesson from these friends' obedience and their willingness to serve (Colossians 3:23–24).

PART 3

❧

Her Passing

The Funeral

L inda passed away on December 3, 2015, fifteen years after her diagnosis. As much as I expected her passing, tears flowed, as I found it overwhelming. The emotional experience of her remains being carried out of the house that day was too much for me to see.

My reaction surprised me. After all, for years I had known this day was coming, and hospice had warned me that the end was just a matter of days away. I discovered that I had hung on to every moment of Linda's life. Her physical passing marked the end of my caregiving and released me. It jolted my emotions. The journey had been so long that it had become my way of life, and that way of life changed in an instant. When you spend seven days a week giving care, and that need suddenly stops, it is a shocking change. Brace yourself for such events.

The best example of this journey's effect on my

family is how one of my grandsons reacted to Linda's passing. At the time, he was only three years old. Think of it. In his whole life of three years, he had only known his Grammie as someone who was lying in a medical bed in a vegetative state. But that was his Grammie.

He entered the house later that day with his parents. As we all sat down at the table for dinner just to be together and support one another, my three-year-old grandson suddenly asked a question. He said out of the blue: "Where is Grammie?" The question stunned us all. He was so young and yet so aware of the change that had occurred. As we adults sat there silently pondering how to answer his question, he climbed down from the table, ran into the other room, and stood right where his Grammie had been for "his whole life". The corner where she had been laying in her medical bed was empty. The bed had been removed and yet he stood there for the longest time. He just stood there and stood there and stood there, staring at the place where Grammie had been his whole three-year life.

My grandson's mother finally followed him and comforted him by saying that Grammie had gone to heaven and that she was okay. That comforting satisfied his little mind, and he came back to the table to make an announcement. As he climbed back into his chair, he loudly announced that Grammie was okay. He said it in such an authoritative way that you could not help but believe him. And then he did something that caught my eye: he picked up his sandwich and finished his meal.

As I later pondered this whole experience with my three-year-old grandson, something suddenly struck me. I could not believe the thoughts that I was having. His actions were a reflection of our journey.

My mind went back fifteen years to when the journey of dealing with Linda's illness started. I remembered that when my wife began to repeat herself, I asked the same question my grandson did: "Where is my Linda?"

The next thing my grandson did was climb down from his chair to investigate things. That reminded me of going into the medical community with Linda fifteen years before to investigate her symptoms.

After that, as he stood there and stood there and stood there, staring at the empty place where his Grammie used to be, I recognized that as mirroring what my family and I did for Linda. We stood by her and cared for her and cared for her and cared for her for fifteen years.

When my grandson was soothed by hearing that Grammie was okay, I remembered my Lord soothing me to give me the strength to care for Linda, one day at a time. And, as he climbed back up into his chair, he loudly announced that Grammie was okay. I knew in that moment that our Lord was announcing to my family through a confident three-year-old that Linda was truly okay. Sometimes, it takes a three-year-old to help you see the big picture. Sometimes, the simple and obvious needs to be emphasized and a three-year-old child is an excellent way to communicate it.

As I mentioned, it caught my eye when my grandson picked up and finished his sandwich. How strange at first that, after all that unusual and significant activity, he simply would go on with his meal. Then, it occurred to me that this is what our Lord expects of us. When such events occur, we should recount them but then go on with our lives. We are not here to be burdened and handicapped by tragedy and difficulty. The time needs to come when we pick ourselves up and "finish our meals," or live out our lives and do whatever God has called us to do.

I shall never forget what our Lord did through my grandson at his tender young age of just three years old. My grandson certainly did not know how significant his simple actions were that day. But to this day, it comforts me to recall this story. It was a gift to me. The innocence of a young child made the experience of Linda's journey and passing that much more impactful. And I am forever grateful to God's Holy Spirit for comforting me that day through one of my own grandchildren as I endured Linda's passing.

Linda's funeral was set for ten days later. I spent those ten days writing a tribute that I wanted to deliver at the funeral. I needed to talk about her in front of family and friends. It was emotional for sure but somehow comforting to me too. Recounting her life soothed me. There were a lot of good things to brag about as well as a lot of thank-yous to say to the many people who had helped us. The full thank-you list was too long to convey, but some were most significant which had to be recounted. I knew Linda would have insisted on thanking as many people as possible, so I listed as many as time allowed.

People came to the funeral from all across the country. So many individuals knew Linda and understood the extremely difficult journey that she and I had made. As I spoke on that day, I recounted many things that were familiar to many of those in attendance. As their tears flowed, so did mine. As emotional as it was, I think it helped us all to hear of the life she lived, how God enabled us to care for her, and how she endured her illness. And the story of my grandson's reaction to his Grammie's passing and of how God's Holy Spirit used my grandson to comfort me on the day of Linda's passing encouraged everyone that Linda was truly okay.

Somehow, the moments of a funeral service do not do justice to a life well spent. That one day of remembering is just not adequate to appreciate a lifetime of achievements and maturing. But life must, of course, go on, so there is no point in dwelling too long. As our Lord reminded me, we humans must "finish our meal" and continue on with all that God has for us to do. Life is so short even though we often speak of how long it seems. In dealing with a life-threatening illness, you are constantly reminded of how fragile and short our time here on earth really is.

We humans have a hard time letting go. To be honest, I do not think we can let go completely.

Grieving sets in as we experience an absence. We have funerals to mark the time when someone is absent, and their physical remains are laid to rest. But Linda's funeral recognized something more important—that she had graduated to an infinitely better place. Clearly, not Linda but Alzheimer's had died! She had been set free of her disease-ravaged body. At her funeral, we celebrated her legacy and rejoiced that she was relieved of this world, with its sin and suffering. The funeral service celebrated not only Linda's life but also the Christian hope that all of us who put our trust in Him shall be reunited one day.

Some in the congregation remarked that their lives would never be the same after that day. More than one couple later told me that the tribute had saved their marriage. Several more said it was a spiritually uplifting experience. Those in attendance requested more than thirty CD's of the service. Our pastor told me afterward that he often uses the CD of the service in his premarital counseling. People were moved by our service that remembered Linda's life and honored God, and that was enough for me.

Finally, a profound sense of relief overcame me as I was freed from my caregiving. I could look back and have no regrets, for I had tried my best to care for her. To me, my caregiving confirmed my love for her, and that comforted me. I considered caring for my wife to be an act of worship. More important, I sensed an approval as I cared for her; I often would sense God's presence. What a privilege it was to worship God by caring for her. It drew me closer to Him as He gave me the strength to complete a life-changing journey.

The whole journey was very difficult but profoundly rewarding in so many ways. To know that the journey is still being referred to and is being used to help others is such a blessing to me. It reminds me that God uses anything and everything in ways that we are not even aware of. Let us constantly do the right thing and leave the results to Him. That way, we will never be disappointed.

The Poem

When Linda passed, I called our children to tell them the news. They were not surprised, but they all were startled by their feelings of loss. Our daughter had been feeling her mother's loss for many years and took the moment to write her thoughts in a poem. It is fair to say that she inherited some of her mother's journalistic abilities.

During the memorial service that we held, it was my turn to give a tribute for my wife. It was my privilege to introduce our daughter to the congregation and call her to the front to read her poem as part of the tribute. The church staff had printed it in the program. I asked the congregation to turn to the poem in their programs and follow along as our daughter read it. Although it was very difficult for her to do because she deeply felt her mother's passing, with great expression and tears, our daughter read the following poem.

Absent

By Christine Lynn Tyson

Through my young years,
the ups and downs,
my mom was always there.
Her presence meant support and love
and always lots of care.

As I grew older, she became my friend,
and she shared her wisdom with me.
She taught me forgiveness and faith in God
and how to love completely.

My wedding came along, and we
together planned it out.
We had lots of fun and special times;
we had much to talk about.
Then that wonderful time arrived
when I would have my firstborn son.
She was so excited to be a grammie;
ahead was lots of fun.

We enjoyed all the young years
as I had more children yet.
But in that time, something was happening;
my mom was starting to forget.

At first, it was the small things,
like where she put her keys.
But then it only got worse.
"God, bring my mom back, please!"

But the disease just kept progressing,
and the rest is a history
of deterioration and sadness,
which was so hard to see.

My friendly, sweet, and caring mom
now lay helpless in a bed.
"We can only do our best to keep her
comfortable," we all said.

The days and weeks dragged on and on;
she slipped away so slow.
She's been absent for so long now,
and I wanted her to go.

I wanted her to be done with this life,
to be free from all her suffering.
So, when I got the news that she
had breathed her last,
I cried but couldn't help rejoicing.
For she has passed from death to life
and has entered that holy place,
forever to live with her Creator
and praise Him face-to-face.

Praise God! Praise God! My mom is back,
and now in heaven she roams.
Praise God she's healed forevermore,
and my mom is finally home.

Now I look forward to seeing her again,
and when I finally do,
I will look her in the eyes
and see the mom I always knew.

She may be gone from this earth,
this world, our dwelling tent.
But now restored, alive in Christ,
she has never been more present.

The scene was very quiet and solemn, as many funerals are. But emotions were very high as we all realized that these words were not just poetic but conveyed a real-life experience. The congregation so appreciated this solemn moment. I had never heard applause at a funeral service before, but this time I did. The poem was a beautiful expression that everyone could connect with. Even the funeral director asked if he could use it in other services of similar circumstances. My daughter said to him, "Of course you may."

This was not a goodbye. It was a rejoicing that Alzheimer's was now dead, but not Linda. It was an admission of her departure and our separation, yet not forever.

PART 4

∽✦✧✦∾

Reflections

These are some of the subjects you ponder
when you care for someone for years on end,
as well as some of the answers I discovered.

Why?

We all ask this question, especially while we are caring for a loved one. When anyone is really sick or in an abnormal state, we wonder why. When tragedy strikes, it hurts us. It turns our emotions upside down. We feel bad, maybe even to the point of tears. We think, *What did I do to deserve this?*

For some reason, we humans need explanations. Nothing soothes our bad feelings like a full and meaningful explanation would. When difficulties strike and we cannot fix them, we are not used to it. If only we could understand and know the mind of God. Instead, we speculate, theorize, and, quite frankly, flounder in our thoughts to help us cope with our difficult circumstances. Think of your difficult circumstance; in my case, the passing of my dear wife.

Imagine my situation. As I would sit next to Linda's bed and hold her motionless hand, my emotions would well up and cloud my ability to cope with what was going on. Her body was dying prematurely. She could not interact with me at all in her last eight years. It hurt. It hurt a lot. To this day, it brings tears to my eyes to remember her journey and my inability to fix it. She was helpless, and all I could do was to care for her basic needs. I wished I could have done more. It drove me to ask, "Why did this happen?" I wanted to know more, so I prayed and asked God.

I found that there is nothing wrong with asking Him. It is an honest question that He understands. I found that asking out of honesty is a healthy thing to do. Unloading my feelings through prayer comforted me. As time went on, my asking turned to anticipation. I sensed that God had called my wife and me to travel a different path than most would. There was a much higher purpose in our life's journey than just living a "normal and healthy" life span. There was a much bigger picture to unfold and an eternal plan that was beyond my ability to comprehend.

Many of us get frustrated when trying to find an explanation for tragedies in life. At best, we can only get a glimpse of the big picture behind our journeys. That's simply because the big picture can span several years and even span several lifetimes. Who wants to wait for that? Our feelings are hurting now. When our lives are turned upside down, we can be so self-centered that we find it very difficult to put our emotions in their place and be open to an infinitely bigger picture. There is a clash between our badly hurt emotions and the long-term benefits of struggles.

We think we should understand the mind of God just as we understand our physical world, but we do not have that capacity. Let's face it: many of us get frustrated when it comes to trying to find an explanation for tragedies. We are just not very good at it. The difficulty seems to stem from our limitations as well as our distractions. We are rather handicapped.

Our five physical senses are so keen that none of us can argue with what goes on in our physical world; we all agree on that rather easily. Also, the sciences continue to discover aspects of our physical world and rapidly expand our knowledge of it. However, scientists have not been able to explore or explain certain unknowns, like life after physical death, the time before the big bang, the improbability of the creation of life, reasons for tragic events, and so on.

Although we are capable of solving many

mysteries of the physical universe, when it comes to eternal purposes, we can get very frustrated and even give up. And worse yet, we often invent philosophies, religions, and belief systems that further confuse us and cloud the issue to the point that we might even ignore or dismiss the subject of eternity. Some humans deal with these unknowns by being atheists. Others turn to agnosticism. Still others let science and the physical world so distract them that they feel no need to venture into what many would call the *spiritual realm*. And for others, if things are going well in your life, then why bother? It can seem like it is not necessary and not worth the effort to venture into spiritual territory.

Further, when some difficulty or tragedy strikes, there usually is no easy way out. We also find it very difficult, if not impossible, to think that all the suffering and tragedy that we endure here in this lifetime has a greater purpose with a positive meaning. Some things are just out of our control. We pray, beg, complain, chase untested paths, and all too often, we are disappointed. We only want what works the way we want it to, and all too often, when tragedy strikes, little works the way we want it to. I experienced this as

I watched my wife deteriorate for fifteen years to the point of her physical death.

I have become rather successful on this earth. Even though I have had my share of tragedies, including my wife's premature passing, I have been blessed in so many ways, but all of that is insignificant in comparison to eternity. I have discovered that God can bring eternal value through difficult circumstances and that our struggling with these tragic events is a very small price to pay for that eternal value. Tragedies are part of our time here, along with blessings and successes. It is hard to imagine but going through tragic events becomes a privilege that we often cannot fully understand today.

I have discovered that only one method can help everyone deal with tragedies. It is a process that has proven itself over and over again. Unfortunately, many will not exercise it, but I challenge everyone to give it a lifelong try. This process is to seek God. He is always there to be found. See for yourself. If you want to know *why*, then seek Him for the answers. There is nothing wrong with asking. Establish a relationship with Him so that everything in your life can be directed for good (Romans 8:28).

Make no mistake, seeking God does require your

effort. Everyone has the ability either to seek Him or not to seek Him. It is a choice of eternal consequences. If you want to know why God has done or allowed something, then seek Him and ask that He direct your situation for eternally good purposes. You may not get specific answers to this inquiry, but you will get answers that change your life and satisfy you. You will be content in knowing Him and trusting that the outcome is under His control. And the reward of that contentment will be a reward that will not only comfort you but also carry you to the end of this life. Seek Him.

As humans, we often struggle to react properly when we face challenges in life. Turning to God is not always our first reaction. Tragedies can so distract us that they prevent us from giving attention to what is eternally important. Do not let tragedies blind you or distract you from what is eternally important. For sure, seeking God is not always easy, but it will be eternally rewarding if we pursue Him.

Humans face several hurdles to seeking God. One hurdle is our skepticism. We all have struggles, some more than others. If you have some tragedy or hardship in your life, then perhaps you are bitter about it and feel skeptical about God's plan. Or if your life has been "normal," then perhaps you are not at all concerned about eternal purposes. Why bother to seek God? But I caution everyone not to be careless about this. You would not be careless with fire, poison, or any other physical danger, so why be careless or negligent with this quest to seek God? You owe it to yourself. The consequence of not pursuing God is much too great. It might just be eternally damning. Your eternal salvation is at stake. Certainly, do not take my word for it. You owe it to yourself to seek God and ask Him to have a personal relationship with you and show you how He can direct your situation for eternal purposes (Matthew 6:33; Proverbs 8:17).

Another hurdle is sincerity. Finding God requires a sincere step of faith, not a shallow experience. If you expect some immediate quick fix change, then you probably will be disappointed. Decide today to give this a sincere try. Then and only then will you succeed in finding God. Sincerity is the key to this whole process. Anything less, and you will not succeed. When you sincerely seek God, you will have no regrets. No one has ever sincerely sought God and not found Him; it always works. He is always there, waiting for your invitation. All you have to do is take just one sincere step toward Him, and He will respond to you.

The final hurdle is time. Humans also have such a hard time with not getting an instant response. If they cannot push a button and make something happen immediately, then they typically have little to no faith in the process. Put your mind into a new mode of just seeking; you are in control of the seeking, not the finding. This might feel strange, but it will free you of worry about the outcome. Please understand that the outcome is really not your concern. God knows what He can do with our situation, so we can rest in whatever the outcome is. He can make the tragic event turn out for eternally good purposes. We humans are only responsible for involving Him, which will help us cope with the outcome and free us of the effect tragedies have on us. Much more important, by seeking Him and forfeiting control, we will be rewarded with finding Him. And, that reward is eternal salvation.

I learned the hard way that seeking is not a time-sensitive process, although we may want it to be. It is a lifestyle. The longevity of His answering often tests the sincerity of our seeking. The positive outcome can literally take years or many lifetimes into the future.

Again, our responsibility is to seek and trust Him. It is His responsibility to reveal Himself to us. The revelation, explanation, or response is totally up to God. That can be very hard to cope with. God is looking for faithfulness to Him. We gain His approval when we show that no matter what the outcome, we will be content. Rest in that, and no matter what circumstances you find yourself in, know that the outcome will be eternally good as long as you seek His involvement. After all, eternal results are all that matter. Our struggling here on earth for a relatively short time is a very small price to pay for an eternally good outcome.

As I cared for and watched my wife deteriorate for years on end, I was deeply tested by this process of only seeking. But I can honestly say that in fifteen years of caring for my wife and fifteen years of seeking answers from God, I received many answers along the way, and many more at the time of her funeral. What a wonderful and gratifying experience it was to hear and see His divine plan as it unfolded over her fifteen-year illness, even though it resulted in her passing. Understanding that so many other lives were positively affected by His plan wiped away all my tears. It would have been worth all our suffering to think that only one person was eternally helped, but it positively changed many people's lives for eternity. What a blessing. What a privilege. What an inspiration. Yes, it was worth it. Yes, it was!

Make the decision today to seek God for the remainder of your time here on earth. Live a lifestyle of seeking and having a relationship with Him. You will not regret it, and you will be able to cope with whatever circumstances you find yourself in, for you will be resting in His care (Jeremiah 29:13).

Application of Seeking God

I n your life, you may experience a difficult event such as a terminal diagnosis, a divorce, a death, a hardship, an imprisonment, a wayward child, an emotional injury, a physical injury, a handicap, adultery, a guilty action, a financial loss, separation from a comfortable state, an unethical behavior, an immoral behavior, a relationship strain, abuse, a disappointment, etc.

Any of these events induces a shock to your system. That shock manifests itself emotionally, mentally, and physically. You feel bad, maybe sad, anxious, or depressed. It can drive you to tears, immobility, or irrational behavior.

In my case, the event was my wife's terminal illness and eventual passing. Because she had early-onset Alzheimer's, the event lasted fifteen years, from her diagnosis to the point of her physical passing. That is a long time for the event to complete, requiring a long time to heal, and perhaps I shall never fully recover during this lifetime on earth. Let's face it; my life will never be the same. I shall never have the spouse of my youth again.

As you ask the question, "Why?" you can only rely on God and continue to seek Him with eternity in mind. That is easier said than done. As I sought Him, I came to rest in the fact that He is in control. Only seeking Him can heal you and encourage you with eternity in mind.

Only seeking Him can satisfy the need to explain your difficulty. And that exercise may only result in a deeper trust in Him, not a detailed explanation of all that has occurred.

Can you get to the lofty state where it truly does not matter to you why certain things occurred? Yes, you can, but that state calls for complete trust in God. You, like I, must seek Him and accept getting there with no timetable in mind and no concern over the outcome. God's purposes in your life will be eternally worth it.

Here is a prayer for you: "Dear Lord, I'm finding it too hard to cope with this situation. In all honesty, I am devastated. I realize that You would not ask me to travel this path unless You were going to help me on this journey. So, I ask that You give me the strength to seek You and trust You for the eternal value of the outcome. Encourage me and give me the strength to walk this path one day at a time. In Your name, I pray. Amen."

When You Die

S everal times over the years, people have asked me about what it was like to care for someone seven days a week for years on end. My answer was always the same, for I realized from the beginning what it was like.

When you care for someone who is terminally ill, you are constantly reminded of the fragility of life. Their condition is so hopeless and desperate that you cannot help but think of eternity. To put it a little crudely, eternity is in your face all the time. You cannot avoid thinking about it and pondering your own mortality. You frequently wonder what decisions you need to make regarding your own life to prepare for what comes after life on this earth.

Our lives here on earth can so distract us that we do not even give thought to the inevitable. We must consider and prepare for life after death. How could we be so naïve? Do you think there is no life after death? Do you really want to take a chance? You certainly do not want to be wrong about the existence of life after death! An overwhelming number of people have had near-death experiences and said that there is a world beyond ours. There is no question in my mind that there is an afterlife. We owe it to ourselves to settle the matter personally and permanently. Do not be so distracted by whatever circumstances you find yourself in that you miss your time here on earth to prepare for eternity.

Human beings, all who have lived, are living and are yet to live, individually make millions of decisions in their lifetime, millions upon millions of decisions. None of those millions of decisions matter for eternity, none of them matter save one; and, when you die, you do not want to be wrong about that one and only decision. When you die, that is not the time to have been wrong about eternity.

If our loved ones who have passed were to come back from eternity and speak to us face-to-face, they certainly would have our attention. The fact that they would be sitting in front of us would startle us into yearning for what they are about to say. I believe that they would convey the three simplest yet most powerful words in all the universe. We need to give our undivided attention to these simple yet all-powerful words. They would say that in order for you to be right for eternity you need to "come to Jesus". Do not dismiss these words because they are cliché or religious or not worth pondering. Consider the following.

You may say that the words "come to Jesus" are too simple to be profound. They are simple for the best of reasons. You see, I don't care whether your skin is black or white or any color in between. I don't care whether you are filthy rich, or you do not have a nickel to your name. I don't care whether you are extremely intelligent and highly educated or you have never seen the inside of a schoolroom. I don't care whether you are tall or short, male or female, young or old, perfectly healthy or terminally ill. No matter what, you can understand the words "come to Jesus". These words are simple so that everyone on the entire planet can understand them; there is no excuse.

And, when you sit next to a terminally ill person, you are constantly reminded of how important these words are. Never make the tragic mistake of thinking that these simple words are beneath your intelligence.

What an eternally tragic mistake that would be. Ponder these words with eternity in mind. They are, simply, eternally important.

These words are all-powerful. I consider them to be the most powerful words in the entire universe. I know, for I called on Jesus in caring for my wife.

The time came when Linda had lost all of her ability to function. Her quality of life had literally dropped to zero. It was about halfway through caring for her when she could no longer walk or do anything for herself. It was about year seven in caring for her when she became bed ridden and totally helpless and dependent. It was the very first night of her being in this state that I remember leaning over her medical bed in our family room. I put my arms completely around her in a tight hug and pressed my cheek against her cheek. I whispered in her ear, "Honey, I love you." I waited for her response, but in return, not only did she not move, but she did not even twitch! My heart sank. All those years of having a relationship with her were now history. She was no longer a partner. She had entered a vegetative state. My wife was gone.

And in that moment, I felt all my emotional strength drain from me. What that meant to me was that I no longer had the strength to continue to care for her. I suddenly realized that I was in an impossible situation. I wanted desperately to care for her, but there was no longer any response from her, and worse, no strength for me to carry on. You see, when you receive no response or appreciation for your care, it becomes far more difficult to be a caregiver. You are giving care for no recognition, no thankfulness, and no reward. I could no longer carry on.

I took my arms from around Linda and tucked her into her medical bed. Then I sat on the chair next to her bed and pondered what had just happened. I felt profoundly helpless and desperate. I did not know what to do. It had become too hard to go on, yet I desperately wanted to care for her to the end. I was between a rock and a hard place. Then, my Christian heritage kicked in. I remembered that with man, so many things are impossible, but with God, all things are possible (Luke 18:27). So, with all my strength I prayed three simple but all-powerful words. My prayer was emphatic. My prayer was very specific. My prayer called for a miracle. With all my strength, I prayed: "JESUS ... HELP ... ME!" It was a prayer most simple and yet most profound that called on the most Powerful in the universe.

I cannot adequately describe with words what happened next. You see I took one step, just one step towards Him, and I quickly sensed that He came—no, He *ran*—the rest of the way toward me and met me where I was. I instantly sensed a great strength come over me, like a steel rod going down my back. I sensed an approval for what I was trying to do. I knew in that moment that I could do another day!! And that was how I cared for my wife another eight years, solely by His strength, which was like manna being metered out daily for me. His help and strength came to me for the next three thousand days, until she passed. It truly was a miracle! People wonder how I could care for my wife for all those years. Simply, He miraculously enabled me.

Coming to Jesus is simple and yet so profound. They are simple words and yet the most powerful words. When you die, you do not want to be wrong. Live your life according to the Bible by inviting Jesus into your life. Believe in Him and you shall not perish. It is not a religion; it is a relationship and a lifestyle. Come to Jesus and be right for eternity.

When Linda was a child, she came to Jesus. On

December 3, 2015, she went to be with Jesus. I would invite you to come to Jesus too. It is eternally worth it! The following Bible verses relate to coming to Jesus.

- **John 3:16 (NIV):** "For God so loved the world that he gave his one and only Son, that whoever believes in him shall not perish but have eternal life."
- **Acts 4:12 (NIV):** "Salvation is found in no one else, for there is no other name under heaven given to mankind by which we must be saved."
- **Acts 16:30–31 (NIV):** "What must I do to be saved? they replied. Believe in the Lord Jesus, and you will be saved—you and your household."
- **Romans 10:9–10 (NIV):** "If you declare with your mouth, Jesus is Lord, and believe in your heart that God raised him from the dead, you will be saved."

ᴄᴏ◉ᴄᴏ

Praying with a Terminally Ill Loved One

Based on Psalm 23

The Lord Jesus is our shepherd; we do not lack anything meaningful. He makes us relax in green pastures and stills us beside quiet waters. He encourages and strengthens our souls in time of need. We are comfortable.

He has helped us throughout life to guide us along the right paths for His name's sake. It has been our privilege to know Him and to live for Him.

Even though we are now walking through the darkest valley, the end of physical life, we will fear no evil, for You are with us. Your rod and Your staff comfort us in this time of great need. Your nearness soothes us.

You have set a table before us even in the presence

of our enemies. You anoint us with oil and bless us with an overflowing life. We are protected and blessed by You.

Surely Your goodness and love will be ours both now and forever, and we will dwell with our Lord and faithful loved ones forever and ever in heaven.

Amen.

EPILOGUE

My journey was a very long and arduous one. That is
not a complaint; that is just what it was.

Miracle after miracle took place as I went along.
To be honest, I think our lives are filled with miracles.
Things that seem coincidental are never so. When you
are a caregiver, you notice them more.

I remember kneeling at my bedside as a teenager,
asking God to guide me in choosing a wife. He gave
me one that I found beautiful in every way. It was my
privilege to have known her. It was my pleasure and
privilege to care for her in sickness and in health. I
have no complaints and certainly no regrets.

I have also prayed that God would use me to
further His purposes. Be careful what you ask for
because the task you get could be very difficult and
yet so rewarding. I do think that God laid Linda's care
in my life's path. It was my pleasure to care for my

soul mate. It was such a difficult yet beautiful thing to do. So much good came from it, most of all God's approval. The satisfaction of knowing that you have accomplished God's will in something is so rewarding in itself. Nothing can take its place. It has eternal meaning.

And now, I am a widower. It is another phase for me in this life. Grieving continues to take its course. Some healing has taken place. Some loneliness has set in. It simply is not possible for me to have the spouse of my youth again, even if I started over with someone else. The finality of that has given me a different perspective.

I have come to realize that complaining about what has happened to me is pointless. You can waste your life being bitter, but that accomplishes nothing. It has been good to have lived on this earth. As I think back on what I have been through in my life in total, I realize that it has changed me in many ways for the better. I have more clarity about what matters in life. I now see a much bigger picture, one that is not so dependent on this physical world. I find it a very comfortable place to be. I wonder what is next or if my eternity is at hand. I shall not know until my life is over. I look forward to eternity, but I also look forward to whatever time I have left on this earth.

Remember, we are not here in these physical bodies forever. Why do we often act and live like we will be? It is so easy to become consumed and distracted by your activities here on earth. Give priority to a much higher calling than just your physical life here. Give of your time, talents, wealth—your all. Everything you do should be an investment in eternity. Seek God, and invest in His purpose, for only that has eternal value. All you have to do is ask Him for a personal relationship and for direction in your life. He will answer you. Just seek Him and trust Him for eternal purposes (1 Chronicles 16:11; Acts 17:27; Luke 11:9–10; Proverbs 8:17; and many more).

Be blessed as you journey together with Him.

APPENDIX

A List for Caregivers

Over the years, I have discovered a number of items that are important in caring for people with Alzheimer's or any long-term illness. This list is by no means complete, but it compiles many points that I consider important to communicate.

1. You must address certain legal issues. At the very least, you should have the following three legal documents on file and update them. These documents are vital to managing your loved one's affairs. You need these documents in order to become appointed as the patient's advocate.

    a. A last will and testament
    b. A durable power of attorney
    c. A medical directive

It surprised me that Linda's doctors first talked to her until she could no longer answer them. They explained to me that legally, they were required to address the patient first before they talked to me about anything. The above documents will enable you to communicate with your loved one's doctor.

2. In order to manage the future with some assurance, you should have the preceding documents in place with others whom you can trust. If something should happen to you, the caregiver, then someone else needs to be able to take over with the authority that these documents afford. For example, if you can no longer manage your loved one's care, then perhaps your children are mature enough to take over, but they need the documents to have the authority to do so. A lawyer who specializes in the writing of wills can help with all of this as well.

3. The first few years of MCI (Mental Cognitive Impairment) are the riskiest. As someone's mental capacity deteriorates, they begin to lose

their ability to manage their lives and make reasonable decisions. Your first concern should be the loss of your loved one's ability to live life normally and rationally. Your loved one might become unreasonable. They might think it is now okay to behave immorally or unethically. They might hallucinate. As they deteriorate, they might do rash things. If you have some assets accumulated, you should consider protecting those assets. Make them less accessible for withdrawal. You do not want to deprive your loved one, but you also do not want them to waste those assets. Plus, if their illness goes long term, as Alzheimer's usually does, you will need those resources to meet their future needs. This is not meant to be a criticism of their character but just a realization of what is happening to them. As a caregiver, it is important that you brace yourself for whatever may happen. Try hard to see the near future. Prepare for it. Your loved one's deterioration will be slow but steady. Remember, the deterioration is not their fault, but it is your responsibility to protect them as well as yourself.

4. You must see the inevitable and have plans in place to react quickly when needs arise. For instance, the day will come when they need supervision, so it is beneficial to research agencies or facilities in your area that can eventually help you with this supervision. Check what kind of care your health insurance covers. If you know all the facts ahead of time, you can better prepare for whatever situation arises.

5. It is important to understand your own capacity for giving care. It is often true that we can do more than we think we can. But as with any other difficulty in life, when we rise to the occasion, we could soon find ourselves in over our heads. The last thing you want to do is burn yourself out; you will become no good to your loved one and also be in severe need yourself by getting depressed, etc. Monitor your health, and have friends or family help you judge your health as well. They can be more objective, looking in from outside your situation.

6. I must also emphasize the need for prayer. It surprised me that one of the first things my wife lost was her ability to pray. That was a very sad

time for me, as it drove home how dependent she had become, even spiritually. I prayed for her. I prayed for myself. I found it very, very meaningful as others told me that they were praying for our journey as well. I truly leaned on our Lord and frequently asked for strength for me and comfort for my wife.

7. I found it very difficult to determine what to do to protect my wife. I saw her ability to drive deteriorate but did not know when or how to curtail or stop her driving. I knew her ability to manage herself was waning, but it surprised me when, one day, she just left the house and wandered the streets. You want to protect your loved one, but you cannot lock them in the house. The best thing to do is to start supervision earlier than you might think necessary. They need someone with them frequently and even full-time. All of this starts sooner than you may think. Try to start supervision sooner rather than later.

8. If you need help during the day so you can go to work or just be off duty as the caregiver, there are day-care facilities that can help you. My wife

did not want to go to a day-care facility, so I did not force the issue. In retrospect, she might have agreed to go had I discussed it with her earlier, when she was more aware. Then, she might have been more understanding and more willing to make the transition to such a facility. I do think it would have been more helpful to her if she had experienced daily interactions with professionals who understood her needs more than a caregiver could.

9. Engage your family in caregiving; they care the most and can also help the most. Our children were very helpful. My wife knew them, and that comforted her. You do not want to burden your family, for they also have their own lives. But they are feeling the loss too, and giving a helping hand now and then will both help them cope with the loss and also give you a break from your caregiving.

10. Early-onset Alzheimer's is considered merciful to the patient. I have to admit that, to my knowledge, my wife never felt any pain. It is fair to say that, in the beginning, our daily interactions were ever changing. But as time

went on, it settled into a very predictable routine. She just came to the point where all she required was just basic-needs care. As sad as that was, it was straightforward, even easy; however, the hardest part was that the kind of basic care she needed went on for thousands of days. The seven-days-a-week routine was very repetitive. The hardest part was adjusting as a caregiver. Those caregiving adjustments over the years were often emotional because every adjustment was a reminder of her deterioration, a reminder of what once was, and a reminder of how much life had changed and of how much it will change as things deteriorate to the end. Understanding the pace and knowing that it may take a long time will help you cope.

11. There are many resources you can call on should you need them. For instance, your doctor and local hospital, the medical research community, the Alzheimer's Association, and your church's staff can direct you. You are not alone, but you do have to reach out. I also found that my friends were very encouraging to me. Just occasionally having lunch with them would encourage me to

keep going. Family, friends, and professionals are all at your disposal. I will say it again: You are not alone. Reach out.

12. When Linda was diagnosed in the year 2000, the medical community thought that there would be a cure for Alzheimer's in ten to twenty years. She passed away fifteen years later with no cure in sight. The search for a cure has been and continues to be feverish. The need is great and is growing larger all the time as our population is aging. Exciting new ideas are being tried in research facilities. Perhaps a cure is near, but no one knows. It is probably safe to say that a cure is possible; we just do not have it yet. It would be important to say that you should not have any false hope. That being said, you should also find out the latest. You might just have the opportunity to enroll your loved one in a clinical trial if you wish. Talk to your doctor and the Alzheimer's Association about such things. Do not give up until you have a thorough and informed answer.

13. As you care for your loved one, remember from time to time that it will all be over one day. Someday, you will look back at the whole

experience. All the decisions you had to make, all the care you had to give, and all the struggling you had to do with the years of straining will be over. You will want to be able to say to yourself that you have no regrets. That perspective will give you strength to do another day, one day at a time.

To Contact Author:

IDOIDIDBOOK@GMAIL.COM